IMAGES

A COLLECTION OF POETRY

VOL. 1

BY
D. MAURICE WADDELL

Images is the first of a number of forth coming volumes of poetry from me, Donald Maurice Waddell (D. Puma). I humbly submit my poems in this first offering and I look forward to sharing more of my work in the near future. I am excited to share this journey with you all. My goal, on this journey that you are about to embark on with me through reading this book, is to paint vivid pictures with my words…. *Images*.

Throughout our lives we've been confronted with images that help us create our reality of everything around us. As do most images, mine come from life, experiences, thoughts, conversations, visions and ideas.

For this first volume I submit to you the various *Images* of love, intimacy, hurt, heartache, as well as life's interludes. My hope is that *Images* will take you on journeys that will paint pictures of various aspects of the love experience……
Touch you in places that you didn't know existed or forgot about…… Show the beauty that lays in you…….Help you look forward to a future of beautiful thoughts, dreams and fulfillment……… Remind you of the hurts and heartaches as well as the loving and tender moments of your journey…… Move you closer to your world of pleasure ……..and finally, I hope that your "Erotic thoughts refuse to subside…" and you *Release*…….. Enjoy

Love, D. Puma

All selections written by Donald Maurice Waddell (D. Puma)

Of Love...

Elusive
Admiring an Angel
This Man
Butterfly
How You Touched My Soul aka "Soul Mate" (A Sealed Letter)
Memories of April
Memories of April (Pt. 2)
We're Dancing
Shelter from the Storm
Tread Lightly
Play With Me
Disclosure
Mira
A Clear View of Unconditional Love
Call her.....Enchantment
Welcome Love
A Dream of My Queen
I Call Your Name
Soul Mate
Eargasms
After Glow
Home at Last/At Peace with My Beloved
Her Name....
I Want to Know Her
She Loves Hard
Whisper Softly
Tequila Sunrise (Help Me Find My Way to You)
Ever Since
Every Word
Summer Soft
Summer Soft (Pt. 2)
Not Enough Time to Say I Love You
The Gig is Up
Moments
Dream
Take Flight...You are No Longer Caged

Of Ecstasy...

Cum for Me
Yummy
Mocha Cappuccino
Wet
Summer
Stealing Happiness
The Shower Scene
The Invisible Woman
Quiet Storm
I Remember You
Say My Name, Say My Name
Unison
The Actor/Type Cast
Impact
Prelude to a Kiss
A Quiet Rain
Honey Cream
Release
Loneliness Revisited

Of Hurt ...

C. L.
Betrayal
Watercolors
What's Love Got to do With It? (The Sacrifice-Pt. 1)
If You Knew
Beatin' My Time
From your Lips
Alone in My Bed
Living a Lie
Next
Thank You
The Worst Kiss
Goodbye
It is Finished

IMAGES

Of Love...

Elusive

It was like that rush you get
When a speeding train goes by
When she walked up to me and removed
Her hair from her eyes
Melodies started to play out in my mind
You know the kind that plays over and over in time
Like the taste of that familiar wine
Or that first time you thought you were flying
It was like that bird would take me on a flight
That would, 'Take me to the sky on a natural high...'
I knew her name
Knew that she would remain
A fixture in my mind
Of the standard a sistah
Would have to reach
To make my curiosity peak
I knew her name
I knew we we're part of the same
Knew she would forever remain
And just like that train
Or bird in the sky
That rush of wind left as it came
As she continued to pass me by

Admiring an Angel

I seek the one I can't have
I desire the one I don't need
And life without is sad
What could it be, what do I see
Don't want to be where I am
Not knowing where I want to go
So much for my plans
Excuse me for wanting you so
Living life among the clouds
But I really don't wish to fly
I live to see your smile
I never want to see you cry
So much I want to say to you
If only you could see my words
The more and more I attempted to do
The more I'm trapped outside your world

This Man...

I can't speak for other brothers
So this is my plea
To express what this man needs

This man needs...A woman
To support me
When the world has taken its best shot,
To be recharged
After the daily battles of a society
Not built to accommodate
But discriminate
A good woman that can soothe me with her thoughts
Warm me with her words
And inspire me with her spirit

This man needs a woman that can love me down
And build me up from the ground
And hold me during a downpour
That can feed my mind, body and soul
With food that satisfies and to help me grow
This man needs a woman who doesn't mind
making love in the rain
Enjoys hearing her body sing
A song, that is free of inhibition
Loving without obligation

This man is not in need of a servant or slave
But a woman that's tailor made
To anticipate my wants and needs
Because a real woman knows that this is the key

This man needs a woman to give birth to seeds,
Gods that are able to see the truth
In what the Creator wants them to be
Not a disciple of mans thoughts and ideologies

This man needs a mate that is self-assured
Her essence, could never be ignored
A woman, not a facsimile
That can do more than 'just be'
Who can see the possibilities and build with broken tools

A woman that can touch the elements of my world by
Making the coldest day warm, and the hottest day cool
Because she knows what every good woman knows
She knows if she follows through,
There is nothing that this man wouldn't do

Butterfly

Carefully I approach…..
My delicate butterfly
Not to startle you
I just want to get closer to you
To hold you, to touch you
So so carefully, I approach you

Carefully I approach….
My beautiful butterfly
With colors pleasing to my eyes
Inviting me inside
Multiple shades of your love
So so carefully, I approach you

Carefully I approach…..
Like warm waves from the sun
Closer, I get to you
I see a reflection of one
You and I as one
So so carefully, I approach

Carefully I approach….
This wonderful site
Not to cage you
Nor to change you
But to find myself in you

Carefully I approach….
This moment in time
Enjoying your rhythm and blues
Enjoying this sweet interlude
Caressing you
So so carefully

How You Touched My Soul aka Soul Mate
(A Sealed Letter)

It was like you touched my soul
When you touched my hand
I looked into your eyes
And saw the truth in various shades of hazel
As if your words about your vision
Was the seal to my spirits' gap
Your visions resounded the answers
I searched for all my life
The vision to be in a relationship...
With the Creator
That will bring you peace and a Soul Mate
That together would produce and nurture seeds
Into Gods to take their place in the Creator's Universe
All moving in synergy to a higher level...
One Love

Not wanting to interrupt you reading the vision
Written on my heart
I listened quietly to the words from your lips
To hear the truth
Your words left me speechless in your presence
As you reached deeper into my understanding
I watched your spirit touch
All in your presence
With a positive force that overwhelmed me with joy...
Your passion and energy
Helped me realize that my vision had not died
But laid dormant until the Queen/Soul Mate arrives
Your words ignited my pledge to be that Soul Mate
Praying each day to make the vision a reality
To move closer to the Creator
To move toward peace
To move closer to
One Love

Memories of April

Magic rainbow skies
Glistened in your eyes
As the birds sung a sweet melody
The sun was on the rise
Flowers realized
The essence of sweetness felt heavenly...
The midnight rain
Brought no pain
As it fell tenderly through the air
The passion like a flame
Could not be tamed
As a common bond was shared...
A period of time
Secured in my mind
That has to be seen as ours
One so kind
Who found the time
To open my heart's door

Memories of April – (Pt. 2)
(The Innocence of You)

Like a sweet oil
You soothed my senses
Your presence rained
Like a melody from
A warm summer night
Innocent yet seductive
Misty yet warm
Your eyes, like a child
Engaged me for love and protection
Your smile, like a warm wave
Embraced me like a lovers' welcome
I accept, but my words were concealed
Inside my flame kindles
For your enchanting aura
My judgment clouded
With thoughts of touching you
With passion
Your touch would reveal the flame
And my reluctance to tame
Would bring forth
An infernal of love, passion,
And seduction of the highest
But of course, I sensed
You saw this when our eyes met

We're Dancing

We're dancing
Five feet apart
Moving to the same rhythm
I long to touch you
To pull you closer to me
To show you what it means to be loved by a man
From holding you in my arms
To gently leading you by the hand
From late night conversations
To form closer relations
To form a creation of a Love Supreme
From that dream
That has been dormant
Until you were sent
But for now
We're dancing
In this Lover's Rock
Three feet apart
Closer from the start
Cautiously moving to the rhythm
I long to touch you
To pull you closer to me
To show you how a man
Can love all the hurt away
While the rhythm makes us sway
Closer and closer
True love only needs a chance
As we continue to dance

Shelter from the Storm

I'm that house that sits in the woods
Secluded and hidden away
On a cold and rainy night
A house that's not meant to be lived in
But to visit,
Take a deep breath
Relax, unwind, stay the night
And when the storm has passed
You continue on to your destination
Or journey
But in the meantime . . . Come in out of the rain
Come out of your wet garments
Seek the warmth of my fireplace
Light the fire, curl up to my bare skin
Feast on the delights of your heart's desire
Shelter yourself with me for tonight, this is your palace
And as the lighting flashes, winds howl, and the thunder rolls
Listen to the music that plays on your beautiful skin
Enjoy and relish the moments stolen
For I will not take what belongs to you if you do not take what is mine
But remember, it's a nice place to visit
This is only a shelter from the storm
You can always feel welcome
When you're on your way to a destination

Tread Lightly

I let you in
And as you journeyed through
You began to see through my eyes
And examined my thoughts
Back then
I couldn't share this with you
Walked through parts of my life
That I keep to myself
Many have took a glance
But were afraid to dance
To the melodies of my heart
But one day you walked in freely
Shed tears for my pain
Stood with me in the rain
Felt my desires
Wants and needs
As you continue to read
Please tread lightly
So not to ruffle the leaves
Or control fate
Just tread and consume
A taste of the sweetness
Of the words that touched you
Savor
Digest it with care
And tread lightly

Play With Me

I need you to balance this seesaw
You know, my go up and down?
Can't you see?
I'm like the child
Sitting waiting for a playmate to play with me
Sitting on the seesaw
On the ground on this go up and down
You keep on passing me by
As I wonder why
You won't sit down
And give this go up and down a try
I promise I won't do it hard
If you don't want me to
Don't mind the others
That you saw on the other side
Some, they tried
But this seesaw needs
Someone who could balance me
Wasn't the right balance you see?
One tried but didn't have the weight
To make me raise
Another had me up so high
That my weight couldn't bring her up
And when she realized the unequal scale
And that I couldn't come down
She stopped coming around
But you seem to have the perfect fit, to balance
My go up and down
Can't you see?
I'm like a child?
Waiting for a playmate to play with me?
You can climb on gently
I will carefully raise you up
You can be on top as long
As you want
I need someone who can
Balance me
Go back and forth
On my go up and down
I promise not to do it hard
Please, sit down?

Disclosure

I held on as long as I could
Probably longer than I should
Fighting to keep the secrets in my heart
Even from the start
With everything in my being
I keep it locked in without you seeing
My inner most self
My inner wealth
What keeps me knowing
And you guessing
What I continue to hide
Then I let you inside
I told you secrets that others searched for
But failed to see with your minds' eye
Beyond the lips
The kiss
The moments of bliss
Full disclosure
Are you sure you can handle it?

Mira

I wish you could see what I see when I see you
I wish you could see my desire to fall into you
I wish you could see our future, our lives
I wish you could see the vision that I see when I close my eyes
Or when I look into your eyes
And see our children
From the endless love we'll make

I wish you could see what I see when I see you
I wish you could see the love that's within me
I wish you could see how you bring out the best in me
I wish you could hear the whispers to my heart when you are near
Or the angels whispering in my ear
Or be there when a song comes on
That describes how I feel about you
"...because I love you, thinking of you..."
If you could see
The love you could have with me
We could began to enjoy what we were born to be

A Clear View of Unconditional Love

Vibin' with a sistah one clear night
She pulled my coat tail to a vibe at the time was beyond my sight
She told me that there was a difference between loving someone and being in love
Being a man of infinite wisdom, I was taken aback but inquired more of what she was speaking of
Love is love, right?
She began to run the different levels of treading waters
There's the love you have for a son or daughter
A love you have for a long lost friend
And love you have for your fellow man
A love that consoles and understands
The love that you feel from the touch of her hand
But when you just love someone, and you can't comprehend
That being in love has the power to transcend
When love transcends the obstacles of time and space
And through differences, heartaches, and difficulties it still can't be erased
When love transcends logic and understanding
And from first look you took flight with no such action as landing
When words aren't necessary to convey
The ability to listen to ones heart from far away
To lay quietly in ecstasy
When caring and sharing happens effortlessly
I remember it now so clear
As the sistah put it in my ear
But I didn't realize until we were falling from a half a mile
That I saw a clear view of unconditional love

Call Her....Enchantment

She sits there
Taunting me
With her powerful stare
In me what does she see?
What does she crave?
My mind, my body, my soul is all I have
And all I wish to save
If I extended my essence, would she laugh?
Or would she affectionately hold what I gave?
Caught between curiosity and fear
I fall deeper inside her enticing stare
With eyes that smile as if heaven-sent
Yes, I'll call her ...Enchantment

Welcome, Love

It's beautiful to finally meet you
After years and years of pursuing you
When I found myself panting from exhaustion
You revealed yourself, increasing my anticipation
So I welcome you with openness
Your warm and secure caress
Love, can you make me a promise?
To keep the sweetness in your kiss
To fall in love with me everyday
To remain with me, and never walk away
To hold me with your strength
To encourage me with your faith
To rub my head in pain and confusion
To rub my head in times of intensity and inclusion
To understand my strengths and weaknesses
To adore boldness and meekness
And all I will extend
My friend
Forgive me if this order seems tall
But you did say that love conquers all

A Dream of My Queen

I had a dream of you
Standing in the sand
The congregation facing the motherland
Dressed in island attire
Looking at each other with desire
This is our wedding day…

As we hear a symphony from the waves
The sun kiss from the rays
Affirming that this is our day
The ancestors condone our love
By whispering through the winds above
And the diamonds that sparkle in the sand
Help blend in our union as woman and man
As we take our proper place
In the Creator's plan
I heard the angels sing in this vivid dream
As you became my queen and I your king…
At First Sight
I approached you and suggested a smooth sweet delicate scent
As your name describes you as a Queen of Mystery
May I inherit the key?
To unlock the mystery that lies behind your eyes?
If revealed, would I survive?
The secrets that you hold behind your sincere eyes?
Carefully I pursue you as you became elusive
Like a butterfly
Waiting to be a part of your world
Share with you the mysteries of my mind
As I whisper your name to myself
Your name flows off my tongue
Like the perfect lyrical riff
Or the sweetest verse that was ever heard
Or like the sweetest sound to ever touch my face
Caught in your essence, I briefly lose my place…
I find myself intrigued
And it's hard to believe
That a light like yours existed
Or a smile like yours would grace me
Or eyes that would touch my soul
Not realizing my heart you hold

I Call Your Name

I couldn't stop your hand
I couldn't push away
You seem to understand
So I let you lead the way
You didn't seem to mind
So I let myself go
Our world seems fine
As my feelings overflow
I'm not in control
Some force has a hold of me
Since then I haven't felt the same
And now and then I call your name . . .

A thought of you on my mind
Brings a smile to my face
You help me unwind
From life's hectic pace
You have undressed my desire
Then designed me with your love
No level was higher
You lifted me far above
I find myself losing touch with time
And at times I feel your touch
You have consumed me
And I've never been the same
Every now and then, I call your name

Soul Mate

My love moves rapidly
Wondering where you could be
Show yourself to me
Garden of…
Let's walk together
The garden is moist tonight
Paradise awaits
Fruit from the Tree
How can you resist
As you call me with your kiss
This moment of bliss
Silent Dancer
Your motion persuades
Unsaid words show me the way
My hunger evades
Mahogany,
Mahogany dreams
I reach for her silently
As she covers us
Heat of Passion/Drippin'
The scent excites me
Triggers my body to crave
Your ocean of waves
Sweet Surrender
Sudden impulses
Evaporates my control
Willingly I gave

Eargasms

I fall into your sounds
And lose myself in your harmonies
Melodies
Flowing through me
How did you know what note to touch?
How did you discover my hiding place?
The soothing tone that pleasures and vanishes without a trace
The further I fall the more you embrace me with your melodious sound
Spinning around, spinning around
I must be falling in love
A slow driving rhythm
Constantly in motion
Solid in time
Steady and sure
Right up to that climatic allure
I close my eyes,
Relax
And let it happen . . .

After Glow

And suddenly, I wasn't afraid
I knew you had my back
Not regretting the love we made
Or the outcomes of the act
And suddenly I feel whole
I knew the rhythm of your heart
No one else could touch my soul
Or keep us apart
And suddenly I found peace
I knew my world had been changed
The chaos in my life ceased
All that was complicated was made plain
In the mist of the after glow

Home at Last/At Peace with My Beloved

I rested on your breast like a child
Secured, warmed, and loved
I take a breath
Released the stress
At peace with my beloved
I close my eyes and realize
That no one can do me no harm
In your arms
Secured, warmed, and loved
I take a breath
Kiss your neck
At peace with my beloved
Sensations of your touch
Bring upon the rush of total submission

Her Name....

She woke up slowly
Each moment she became brighter and brighter
Warmer and warmer her rays touched my soul
Watching her I began to thank the Creator
        for his greatest creation
And for letting my eyes see her in her fullness
        her beauty, her first glance
Waiting all night just to see her face
Watching her sleep all night
Being careful not to wake her too soon
Staring at the moon, covering her like a blanket
I hear the air whisper her name…
And as I watch her I imagine her soft kisses,
        anticipate her warm embrace
And await the love she will bring when she awakes…..

I Want To Know Her

I see her
Dancing
Eyes that smile
Hair wrapped in cloth
Material complimenting her curves
Cowrie shells around her ankles
Dancing
Rhythmically to the sounds of the drums
My mind slows her pace
Pursuing her every move
I see her
Movements of an African Goddess I once knew before
When we walked on the sands along the coast
And dialogued about our understanding of our universe
Our conversations with the blades of grass
Revealing the secrets spoken in the wind
Unveiling that you weren't known by another
And like children we laughed and played in the calm blue waters
Reflecting as we watched the stars glimmer off the ocean
And as her movement captured real time
Her eyes met mine
And her hello gave the presence as if she knew me from another time.

She Loves Hard

I can imagine her telling me that she loves to wear my essence
After we make love so she can keep my scent with her all day
And I can imagine when she holds me it's so tight as if someone
was trying to take me away

I can imagine... She loves hard...
Harder than I ever been loved in my life
and at times I would think it's psychotic
But then find it erotic
And it would excite me to think that one day
I could make her my wife

I imagine that she loves that hard
With reckless abandon
Her love so demanding
And at times I would find it hard to keep up
But as her man I would stand
Toe to toe, blow for blow
Like a title bout
Because I know that this lover's rock is worth every ounce,
Of blood, sweat, tears, snot, everything I got, to keep her satisfied
Loving me as only she could

I imagine she loves hard....
Like the ratta-tat-tat of a baseball bat
Upside the dome and reminds me
Constantly that no matter where we are
We are at home as long as we love without fear,
Without conditions, without regrets and as long as I live
And in the afterlife, and in the after after life, and in the after after after life,
And in the after after after after life after that......
There will never be anyone that loves me this hard....

I imagine......she would ......love me that hard

Whisper Softly

Whisper softly
Let it surround me
And blanket me with warmth
Arousing my creativity
You essence engaging mine
Coming together like a puzzle
Like a sweet blush of wine
And as fallen leaves rustle
I imagine your kisses…

Whisper softly
Let it caress me
Like the candle embraces the flame
Constantly, gently
Like the melodious tempo of rain
Kissing the sky, in the still of the night
Memories of you holding on tight
As you whispered ever so softly…

Whisper softly
Only you and I can hear
As our moist skin blends
Free from fear
The pain of the past mends
All is forgiven
Silence sounds so sweet
As our spirits meet
Whisper ever so softly my love

Tequila Sunrise (Help Me Find My Way to You)

Waiting for the clouds to clear
Waiting for your warm rays
Wanting to be intoxicated by your stares
Like taking shots of Patron
Until we moan
Until I hear your soft whispers ...*Papi*
Until our fears disappear
Wanting to taste you
Feel you
Wanting this feeling you've given me to stay
Wanting you to feel my love
View my world
Imagine the possibilities
Wanting to help you see the vision I see
So vividly.....
Waiting for you to touch this vision with me
Wanting to hold it together
Like a new born child and nurture it
With the intensity
Of stolen moments.....
That replay in my mind
Wanting so much for you to be mine....
To look into your eyes
To enjoy every tequila sunrise......

Ever Since

Ever since you touched me I thirst but can't get enough
Suddenly I'm not afraid to trust
I saw your face and from that moment I knew my heart was gone
Your eyes held me as your voice flowed through me like a song
Thoughts of loving you filled my mind
And before I could grasp it I lost track of time
Sipping your passion, basking in your glow
In your mistful world where moments move ever so slow
Directed by your presence, always there to console
Captivated by your soft body, come let me hold
Your closeness I absorb
Your nectar I adore
And I danced in your thoughts
By your beauty I've been caught
So alluring, so intense
And I have been yours ever since

Every Word

From the night I confessed, I Love You
As the coldness of the summer breeze blew
When we danced and giggled like children
And pledged to be friends to the end
Bedroom picnics
Midnight kicks
Sounds of silence as we floated effortlessly
As if we were lying on a leaf floating in a pond
As we talked, cried, shared
Laughed, loved, and cared
As we stood as a team against everyone . . .
Know that every word spoken
Can never be broken
Every word,
Every word

Summer Soft

Thoughts of Brown Sugar
On the tip of my tongue
Remembering the way you moved
The sweet song you sung
Descendant from the mother
That we are all from
You touched me with your
Warm rays all summer long
Thoughts of Honey Dew
Dripping all over my face
I remember every drop
I still savor the taste
Just the smell takes me back to that place
How sweet and sticky it was
How could my mind ever erase
Thoughts of watermelon kisses
On the full of my lips
The way you walked over and moved your hips
The way you filled your cup and I took a sip
In a pool of your melon juice
Where I took my first dip

Summer Soft (Pt. 2)

Soft as a summer moment
As my eyes open
To find you next to me
Rays of your presence
Bless me
With the feeling
Of unconditional warmth
Experiencing that perfect taste of you
Savoring
I smile
Because I'm where I should be

Cold as winter
As I think of the fight today
As I think of what lies outside
Leaving this place
Jumping in the rat race
Put on my game face
Battling armor
And the weapons I could carry
For the battle
But even the greatest of warriors
Need to be replenished
So I long for those soft summer moments

Give me
Replenish me
Remind me what I'm fighting for
Why I brave the outside
Make it worth going through all this
To find a pleasant place in your eyes
Help strengthen me
And I will take on this fight daily
To bask in the soft summer moments
With you
Loving me
Healing me
To fight through another cold ass day

Not Enough Time to Say I Love You

It's not enough time to tell you what your love means to me
Or what your love has allowed me to see
It's not enough time to express to you in words, love making,
Song or gifts …
It's not enough time to explain why the tears stain my face
Or why I can no longer return to my original place
But as the arid wind ran across my face
I made an attempt to escape myself
To relieve the pain
But the memory remains
Wishing that we met in a different life
Is the recurrent thought I fight
The brief romance that seemed to last a lifetime with you
Was not enough time to say,
 I love you

The Gig is Up

I never met anyone like you
My facade fell through
What took a lifetime to put into place
In one day, you were able to erase
Faced with all my flaws
I feel the need to change
The truth was never there
Exposed I feel so strange
And all this time the facade was real to me
And like a religion I believed it to be true
So blinding even I couldn't see
And at one glance you knew
My reality was never true
….Damn you…..

Moments

There are moments
Where I found myself
And instances
Where I lose myself
When I share
And when I fail to care
Moments of truth
And lies
Moments wishing for tomorrows
To escape past sorrows
Moments of love, joy, gladness, passion
Moments of sorrow, pain, fear, and sadness
Ever present that my moments are but a wink of an eye to the
most high
Experiencing each moment
Until our meeting in the sky

Dream

I never stopped talking to you
I never stopped thinking of you
I never stopped praying for you
Dear friend you were there to mend
I was there as a friend
To encourage each other through our plights
Honesty was our creed
We were both in need
Of someone who would listen
We fell in
Where have you been all my life?
Were you the one I was supposed to wait for?
I swore
That I would not stop talking to you
But I told you that the Creator
Had a plan for you
In your plans it was shown that I was not included
I was excluded
Because I tasted what was forbidden
Hurt feelings remained hidden
Selfishness took over
Refusing to hear the order
I indulged and held you captive
From predestined fate
Until the voice became too loud
Your vision too bright
Dream, your future awaits

Take Flight . . . You Are No Longer Caged

I didn't like the way you were
So I set out to capture your heart
With my prose I attempted to lure
In a golden cage of love to keep you caged
To admire, cherish, and guard
To feed you seeds of love
To watch you grow
Soaring far above
To bask in the afterglow…
Anticipation of your brilliant flight
Somehow I lost sight
The more I held you close
The less chance you had to be
My lack of vision stunted your growth
Suddenly I began to see
The pain and hurt I cause by keeping you caged
Now I know why the caged bird sings…
What to me was a song
To you was a cry of longing
Being locked in a fit of rage
And even when it was joy I intended to bring
The timing was wrong
But the bond remains strong, God willing
So finally you are free
May your journey be sweet
Remember when the clouds prevent you to see
Always know your heart is secure with me
Release the rage, Take flight. . . You are no longer caged

IMAGES

Of Ecstasy...

Cum For Me...

Heaven awaits us
Let your rain fall on me
As you ride gently

Yummy

Drippin' all over my face
Neck, chest, hands
Sticky cotton candy
Fudge marble swirl
Dippin' my finger into
your sweet pot to taste
Slowly runnin' down my hand
Would you like some?
Don't be afraid
Taste it, it's yours
Don't you dare take this
sweet buffet away
I have a taste for strawberries
So unlock your strawberry patch
And every drop I will catch
Everyday is your birthday
Candy Cane
Can you stand the rain of passion
Coming your way
Sweet sugar gumdrops
In your eyes
Under your brown sugar sunshine
Spreads its beautiful rays
Overwhelmed by your sweet warm haze

Mocha Cappuccino

I saw you, and immediately forgot my name
You turned around like some scene in a movie
Time stopped
My mouth dropped
An epiphany came across my mind screen
All the others have been
Preparing me for you
The games
The pain
The losses
The gains
The sun
The rain
The wild
And the tame,
Was just a mere preliminary
To the pleasure of you

Fuck the spoon
I'll just drink you down
Slowly and…
Consume the sweet
Richness of your taste
Your smell
Your texture
Warm and soothing
Setting off sensors in my brain
That signal… I have to have you!

Fuck the cup
I'll just lick you up
Right where you stand
Down on my knees and hands
Please find it in your plans
To make me your man
And stir me slowly
Mocha Cappuccino
Into your coco, milky, smooth, and steamy
Mixture
Until we are one
Mocha Cappuccino

Wet

This should be filed under: **WET**
Candles around the tub
Lighting the bathroom
The appearance of Gold
Misty...
We are both in the state of mind
Where no one exist behind the blinds
Covering you with sweet water
Silk in its texture
Dripping down in slow motion
Like a scene from a movie
Only this time
There are no retakes
No cameras
Just candlelight,
This warm bubble bath
And you...
Action...

Feeding you fruit from my wine glass
And later we can make gentle waves
In our sensual pond
The scene colors your skin gold
As the mystery of you unfolds
Tenderly
We make love
With the scent of vanilla
Floating softly in the air
You and I unaware of the angels
That watch over us
While we continue to spin in our sphere of passion
Wet
So tell me ... how's the water?

Summer

As my body pressed
Your moist sweet flesh
The scent of you
Excited every inch of me
The descending sun
And the evening breeze
Could not stop the beads
Of sweat from dripping
Your sweet place calls
I touch it
Again and again and again
I come ... to it willingly
Receive me ...
Quench me ...
Feel me ...

Stealing Happiness

As I showered you with rose pedals
And laid you down in the place where they fell, I watched
The pedals feather your skin
I couldn't help but to feel that you were meant to be, in this secret garden
Wanderlust through your fields,
I close my eyes and my mind was unlocked
To watermelon kisses and candy rain wishes
Roped in your passion
I was compelled to stay in your bondage
Finding myself kissing and licking where the creator had
given you to nurture
Watching you pleasured, watching you fulfilled
Mentally videotaping every touch, sense, smell,
moan, movement
Moments of intensity as if we were at war
In pursuit of possession of each other's warm territory
We both surrendered as the white flag is waved
Signifying the end of our lovers duel
Finding it hard to explain the tears we shed
And as our tears descended from our bodies
on to the rose pedals
We held each other tighter as if we were waiting for the storm
that might distance us
But our fears soon subsided as we shared kisses
And at that moment we seem to come to the conclusion that
Our fate was sealed
And resigned to live for the moment
Until our fate was revealed

The Shower Scene

As I watched the water cover your body
I find myself touching the places
Outside this scene that would be revealed
And as my thoughts are running through the episodes of love making
I kiss you softly and caringly, as sweet ripe fruit
Being watered by
Sweet juices
My skin feels
Dissolved with yours
Enmeshed and engaged
By the long wet kisses
Feeling the water run through your hair
Down your back
I savor you…

As my organ of taste
Anticipates love
Drops from your nipple
Unable to wait
I initiate with slow circular strokes
Creativity occupies center stage as
We fulfill our erotic desires
A scene, which seems
To play out for years
As the water acts as
An aphrodisiac
And washes away our fears

The Invisible Woman

Your man don't know why you wear that sundress in my favorite shade,
The love we made
Or the treasure I found
As I surveyed your mound
He doesn't know the meaning when you arch your brow
When he says something foul
And why you don't trip when he's out all night with his boys
Or why you're not interested or annoyed
He sees you but hasn't noticed a difference in your walk, your attitude
Or how I brought out the woman in you
To him, things remain the same and you haven't given him a clue
He still thinks he has control over you

Your man thinks he can predict what you do
What you say, how you feel
He don't know that I'm the one you come for and to;
I be laughing at that nigga, for real

Blind to the fact that I'm the one you dream about
Think about, yearn for
The one you want inside you

Your man thinks all the bases are covered
But left home base wide open
And you received me
As if this is my rightful place
And without leaving a trace
Tracking across your curves
You savor the sincerity of my touch
The scent of my skin
The softness of my eyes
While your sweet nipple is in the center of my mouth
You receive me willingly
And as you close your eyes
Softly a tear rolls down your face
As you savor the taste
Then suddenly you awake
And secretly smile about your brief escape
Until the next time......

Quiet Storm

Lying here with you
I hear the rhythm of the raindrops
I feel them in my heart,
One by one as I touch you
Moving to the rhythm as we make love
The raindrops seem to intensify the passion shared
Wet juices cover us
As if we were the source of the Quiet storm
That effortlessly passes over us
Calmly, passionately, effortlessly
Moving across me
Rain on me
Never mind getting wet
Nor will I ever forget
The rumbling of your clouds
The rolling of your thunder
And your teardrops on my chest as we rest

I Remember You

Remember?
After dark, in the park?
We made love as you climbed the fence?

Remember?
Making love
And I made you salute twenty-one times
Happy Birthday
Remember?
The back seat of jeep
We swung an episode
The secrets you told
Remember?
Losing your breath
Making love, hot sex
Getting so wet
Your down pour of sweet rain
All over me
Remember?
Me singing to you
Speaking in tongues
In a language only you could interpret
When we broke in
You new place
Body to body
Face to face
The pressing
The moisture
The taste
Remember?
When you see me
Do you remember?
Do you remember?
I remember you

Say My Name, Say My Name

She calls my name
As if she created it
Like sweet rain
As it leaves her lips
Like God touched you
With his presence
I see the light in you
That glows from your essence
Say My Name...
To unlock
What you stored in me
The precious stock
That you find at the heart of me
Like the warm waves that cover me
Never depleting
But completing
Leaving a dry valley
Overflowing with the juices of you
Say my name

Unison

You're inside of me...
Yeah, deep inside of me
Holding your heart beat
As if I hold my very own
Feeling your warmth even when I'm alone
Yet I'm never alone
I feel so high
Yet as Icarus was instructed
I must maintain a balance
Not to fall in the sea
Yet, in my heart and my mind there's no doubt
that if I decided to lose myself in you and
soar toward the sun...
You would catch me
As the rays melted my wings away,
You would be there to
Save me...
Love me...
I feel your touch when I touch,
I feel your kiss when I kiss,
I feel your heart beat when I feel my own,
As I enter you I feel you enter me,
I feel your pain when I'm in pain,
I feel your love when I love,
I want when you want,
I need when you need,
I'm there where you are,
And you are where I am,
You're inside of me...
Yeah, deep inside of me

The Actor/Type Cast

Like an actor that is type cast in a role
I rattle off lines
As naturally as I breathe
So naturally that it touches your soul
I tell you what you want
I tell you what you need

The leading ladies change
And the stories are sometimes strange
But what was once an act
Turns into real life, tight and exact
Unable to expose my other talents
I run off lines
As naturally as I breathe
I tell them what they want
I tell them what they need

To be myself,
That's out of character
To play the role for you is more comfortable,
more familiar
The lover, the funny man
From being baby to Superman
Play off Broadway
While others move on to bright lights
I am used to moving others to stardom
Remember, you are no longer caged … take flight
I run off the lines
As naturally as I breathe
I tell them what they want
I tell them what they need

Impact

At first impact
Or bodies clashed
Like magnetic forces
Destined to collide
We performed the act
Our passion, finally unmasked
As free as wild horses

Prelude to a Kiss

Like a flame
I burn with the desire to touch your lips
Secretly you envision the same
My heart flutters a bit, I must admit
For just the mere thought of the act
Unlocks the barriers of my physical control
In fact, every touch fulfilling and exact
Flashes of ecstasy before the moment unfolds
Every sense, every sensation
The silent anticipation
As we slowly open our hearts' gate
Our windows to the world close as we partake . . . and taste.

A Quiet Rain

You came like a quiet rain
No one predicted it
No one saw it coming
No one was able to feel it
But you and I
Unassuming yet refreshing
And as we laid there
Motionless
The air seemed to cool us down
And dry any traces of our encounter

Honey Cream

Honey Cream, it seems that I can't get enough of your sweetness
Every sense arose, and chose you when we first met
Sweeter and sweeter flows the flavor of your kiss
A richly laced flavor that dips . . . ever so slow from your lips
Glaze me with your out pouring of kindness
Cover me with your heavenly bliss
Soak me in your magnificent grandeur
Amuse me with your contagious laughter
Tease me with your pleasing smile
Embrace me with the luster of your love
Give more than that which is allowed
More than one can speak of
For I am addicted to your nectar
And have been captured by your lure

Release

Our bodies
Thrusting at a feverish pace
Animalistic cries
Both face to face
Sharing the same skin
No thoughts of ending
This duel
Just wildly wading in this pool
Of juices
Erotic thoughts refuse
To subside our synchronized
Thrusting
Dime mas
Dime mas
Duro, duro
Entonces...Soltar

Loneliness Revisited

I miss walking through your wet grounds
Your passionate sounds
The distinguish scent of your juices
Wearing you like a necklace
Dreams cannot suffice
Being the only in your eyes
The warmness of your thighs
Your smooth path that guides
Wet with your nectar
Flows wherever you are
Speaking in your foreign tongue
Remembering what a beautiful song you sung

IMAGES

Of Hurt ...

C. L.

Can this be true?
Am I really here with you?
A love supreme hidden in a celestial kiss
Never before have I felt like this
Primal Sounds of passion accompany an orchestra of nocturnal bliss
As my mind and body commence to submit
There I go, There I go, There I go
As you made love like an angel
Something once thought forbidden
Melts away when I gave in
Could it be your hazel eyes
Your moist thighs
The sincerity of your caress
Or your extracting of my essence
Smoothing your edges with my thoughts and dreams
I feel your energy flowing through me like a vigorous stream
Trying to photograph this moment like a child
My third eye began to run wild
Thoughts of absorbing you ran through my mind carelessly
All I could envision was endlessly, you and me
But sadly you began to envision negatively
And saw that we weren't meant to be
Despite your heart and soul's longing for my presence
And suddenly perfection was lost before given a chance

Betrayal

And at that moment I felt cold
Something inside took flight, but yet I'm not free
The summer's heat couldn't fill the emptiness from the heart that was sold
Stolen recklessly from an enemy unseen
Time effortlessly seemed erased
My memories are difficult to trace
As my trespasser's deeds are played out before my eyes
And instead of turning away, I'm guided to accept this fate
For, long ago, I set the table that awaits
But all words escape me but why
The path must be journeyed
Despite the fruitless endings
Until I find the road less traveled

Watercolors

As tears drop from my eyes
The world seemed to be painted of watercolors
What was clear is now slurred
And as the blue sky fades
The canvas seems jaded
As you seem to fade in the tapestry
Through the blur I see why this has to be,
Why it can never be just you and me

What's Love Got To Do With It?
(The Sacrifice-Part 1)

What the fuck was I thinkin' 'bout?
As I tried to pull the words back in my mouth
Come to think of it, I never asked
But as always you twisted my words like a drunk with a flask
Before I was aware
I was here
Hurtin' the ones I adore
Because in my eyes lies a locked door
That won't allow entry anymore
It must remain protected for it's the core
I lost sight of the key
Behind the door lies the will to trust or be
The lovin', carin', person they saw in me
Instead of openin' up I flee
And sit curled up as if I was a child of three
Not allowed to be free
You stifled my muse
But I stand accused?
How could you love when everyday you're destroying me?

If You Knew

If you knew how much
Your lies hurt my ears
You would remain silent; for fear
That you would speak your fears
Into existence
Exposing the truth

If you knew how much
My heart feels the nail
Of every act of betrayal
That you try to conceal
The guilt that you feel
If you knew how heavy
My eardrums beat
When you think of the heat
Of a love you decided to squander
You wonder…

But if you knew
What kind of love surrounded you
Your happiness could have reigned
And eliminated your pain

Beatin' My Time

After we made love
I had the strangest feeling
That you were making love to someone else
Whose arms didn't feel like mine
Whose lips taste of a different wine
Who's skin was softer
Who's body was warmer
After we made love
You just turned away
You couldn't look me in the face
But your smile said you were in another place
And what's deep
You were the first to go to sleep
But the tell-tale sign that things weren't the same
Is when you came
You called out her name

From Your Lips

Conversations in your sleep
Told me of your actions of deceit
The whisper of his name
From your lips it came
The smile on your face
Told me that I had lost my place
You told me that you would be true
Your sub-conscience came through
And made an honest woman of you
But you never knew
I guess it's true that your body reveals
What you try to conceal
In your attempts to fulfill
I could no longer feel
Your lies to my ears bring pain
As you try to explain
But no clue
What your sub-conscience did to you

Alone in My Bed

You lay next to me
But I'm alone in my bed
You see me
But you rather talk to your girlfriend instead
Find anything to occupy your time
To you everything comes before me
Fail to realize that this man is at his prime
And that years ago I set you free,
Set you free from the responsibility of making love to me
Taking care of me
Sharing hopes and dreams with me
Being a lifelong friend to me
I freed you from probing my thoughts
And it's beyond me
How you refuse to see
Or understand
That you failed to keep this man
Instead
You try to hold on
As I lie alone in my bed

Living a Lie

What are we making
If we're not making love?
Are we taking, without the consideration of...love?
Emotionally, not into you
Physically, you're there
So would the act be true?
Despite the fact that you would be unaware
So what would we be making
If we're not making love?
What would I be taking?
What crime would I be guilty of?
Would it be a crime to say I love you
When my heart doesn't feel the same?
To pretend I'm happy
To cover the pain?
Would the creator view it as a sin
To tell you I love you
Without feeling that within?

Next

Surprise!
In your eyes
As you were a witness
To my resurrection
Nothing short of a miracle, confess
You were the planner of my destination
A confused smile you wear
And through you I stare
How dare you pretend
Your mind presence offends
Foe or friend
Simple to comprehend
But your brain can't compute
That I'm striving for harmony, not a dispute
God bless the child
That truly had his own

Your fury of negativity ran wild
But I was able to hold on
Despite your attempts to do the nasty to my mind
To rage mental Vietnam on my mind
Left your world behind
Chasing three blind mice
And you question my manhood or intelligence
I don't think so
You're not worthy
Or have the authority
To sit on that seat
Nor can you penetrate
The mind set regardless of how wet
Or spiritually, physically, or mentally tall enough to reach my
level of consciousness…
And while you're only using three percent of your brain
I'm sitting on the outer realm of existence
Creating time,
Courting immortality

Thank You

It has been a long time
Since I've heard from you . . .
You've come to mind from time to time
Yet I found my way over you . . .
You made the choice
And let me walk away
Now regrets in your voice
And you want to have my baby?
Despite the time that passed, you seemed to have remained the same
But the bumps and curves of life has helped me change
And you're speaking to me as though nothing has changed
Everything is forgotten
As if we spoke to each other yesterday
Like a flashback in the movies the memories come back to me
Sometimes we learn hard lessons in life
My lesson was learned well
Back from the flashbacks, I listen to you contradict yourself
Fearing your time was running out
You appeared unsure of yourself
Oh yeah, it's all coming back to me
I remember why I had my doubts
It's funny how the bumps and curves of life have helped me gain
It seems silly to me now, I thought I was in pain
No struggle, no progress
I guess . . . I should thank you
For helping me grow into the fine Afrikan man that I am
Because if it wasn't for you
The journey I could never understand

The Worst Kiss

Can't remember the season
But for whatever reason
The air was ice cold
Our eyes met and the tears flowed
Not from happiness you see
But the pain we inflicted senselessly
The surroundings seem vague to me now
As I remember
Words stop coming to my mouth
They took the silent route
To my mind
Voices inside my head
Echoed the things that you said
And like a child I stared
Giving no indication I cared
Your eyes saw me pause
And offered solutions to help my cause
Even you began to see that I was beyond the power of you
You held me as if to say
'Stay'
But my heart had long moved away
Sensing this, you said goodbye with the softest kiss
My last taste of bliss
And the worst kiss I ever knew
Was my last kiss from you

Goodbye

You kissed with lips that lied
But you won't see me cry
Although I hurt inside
I won't sit and agonize
You touched with untrue hands
But you don't understand
How I can have intuition...
Not included in your future plans
You looked with eyes so cold
I knew but never told
Touches couldn't console
I guess some things you can't control
You spoke with shallow words
But every word was heard
Although you didn't have the nerve
You taught a lesson well learned
You won't see me cry
Because now I have the strength to say goodbye

It Is Finished

Thinking back
It was quite sad
Trying to invest in a love you never had
Trying to change your twisted fantasies
In your warped sense of reality
All the while disturbing the peace
Until I decided to cut the leash
Nights I used to hope and pray
that you wouldn't touch me...
You, wanting to hold me with your unbathed body
As I continued to take giant steps
Away from your tangled net
Your tortured soul
Your bottomless hole
You never loved yourself
So how could you love anyone else?
Only in this for you
And you thought I couldn't see through
But I had a clear view

Never a friend
Never a lover
Never a comforter
Or mate
But mastered the art to aggravate
I continue to flow
You can't let go
Carried the cross
I guess it pleased you to bruise me
Use me
Father why have you forsaken me
But never thought I would rise in three
End of story
It is finished.

The greatest poem has never been written...
Since it's trapped inside my mind, for all time...
God whispered it to me in my deep sleep...
And gave it to me alone to keep...

Thank You........

The Creator (The creator and source of my life): All praises to God which all blessings and mercy flows. Thank you for having mercy on this sinner. If I had ten thousands tongues...you know the rest. Nobody but you...

David E. Waddell (Daddy): Thank you for everything, especially making me walk instead of having people carry me. Thank you for the lessons, vision and guidance, Love you Pop.

Delores Waddell (Mama): who told me that this would happen.....thank you. Thank you for all your encouraging words and love. I wish you could be here to see the seeds that you planted grow. I miss you...

Jamila and Dakari (The Seeds): thank The Creator for the gifts he sent in you my seeds. You keep me going and are my reason to come out swinging every day. Remember the lessons....

To Angela and Charlene: Thank you for your time, patience, and wisdom on this project. I thank the Creator for bringing us together to complete this.....

There are just too many of you to thank. Here we go... Instead of naming names, you guys get in where you fit in. To all those who read and gave me your seals of approval and pushed me to keep writing; you know we do what we do to survive. Family and Friends who were there and are there in the struggle; don't they know that we're built for this? Family Friends that know my story; who could ever imagine this? Uncle Fred and Aunt Ernestine who saved my life. Those who are no longer here especially Rosa Lee Woods who's prayers for me are still in God's ears.

To those who tried to bring negativity to my life, my sincere thank you. Without your energy this would not be possible. Things that you did that were meant to hurt me, The Creator used it to help me succeed.....

Bio

Donald Maurice Waddell was born in New Haven, Connecticut. He is a writer, comedian, instructor, and radio host of The Urban Jazz Connection. He began writing at the age of 14, after taking a creative writing class in his sophomore year in high school. While in this class, Don knew he had found his calling. Many recognized his talent for writing poetry and soon he began compiling volumes and volumes of poems. "It started with writing song lyrics to music that I would hear in my head. These lyrics soon became poems."

When asked where he gets his talent for writing he states, "I believe that it's a gift from the Creator and I am humbled to be able to use it to touch the lives of others...."

Donald Maurice Waddell is an Alumni of Wilberforce University and The University of Chicago. He currently resides in Chicago, Illinois where he teaches Social Work practice at Northeastern Illinois University.

www.ingramcontent.com/pod-product-compliance
Lightning Source LLC
Chambersburg PA
CBHW071841020426
42331CB00007B/1815